JUL 99

KN

THE **7** CONTINENTS

ANTARCTICA

APRIL PULLEY SAYRE

TWENTY-FIRST CENTURY BOOKS
BROOKFIELD, CONNECTICUT

Thanks go to our reviewers: Beth Clark, of
the Antarctica Project, Dr. Arthur Hirshorn,
and Lesley Keogh.

For John Ballard, Elizabeth's proud papa,
and her grandparents Jim and Nancy.
Welcome to the family tree!
—A.P.S.

Published by Twenty-First Century Books
A Division of The Millbrook Press, Inc.
2 Old New Milford Road
Brookfield, Connecticut 06804

Library of Congress Cataloging-in-Publication Data
Sayre, April Pulley.
Antarctica / April Pulley Sayre.
p. cm. — (The seven continents)
Includes bibliographical references and index.
Summary: Describes unique characteristics of the Antarctic continent including
its landscapes, geology, weather and climate, coastlines, air and
soil as well as its plants, and animals.
ISBN 0-7613-3227-8 (lib.bdg.: alk. paper)
1. Antarctica—Juvenile literature. [1. Antarctica.] I. Title.
II. Series: Sayre, April Pulley. Seven continents.
G863.S25 1998
919.8'9—dc21   98-27264
                                                              CIP
                                                              AC

Printed in the United States of America
1 3 5 4 2

Photo Credits

Cover photograph courtesy of © B. & C. Alexander

Photographs courtesy of Photo Researchers: pp. 8 (© George Holton), 14 (© Simon Fraser/SPL), 20 (© Doug Allan/SPL), 28 (© Carlos Goldin/SPL); B. and C. Alexander Photography: pp. 16 (© Hans Reinhard), 30 (© Paul Drummond), 36 (© Hans Reinhard), 40 (© Paul Drummond), 44 (© Ann Hawthorne), 47 (© Ann Hawthorne), 50 (© B. & C. Alexander); Peter Arnold, Inc.: pp. 18 (© Doug Cheeseman), 56 (© Kim Heacox); Extreme Images: p. 24 (© Jonathan Chester); Minden Pictures: pp. 26 (© Frans Lanting), 34 (© Flip Nicklin); © Wolfgang Kaehler: pp. 12, 27, 32, 48.

CONTENTS

Introduction   CONTINENTS: WHERE WE STAND   5

One   GUIDE TO THE BOTTOM OF THE EARTH   9

Two   ANTARCTIC ICE   15

Three   ANTARCTICA: IT'S REALLY COOL!   21

Four   LIFE IN THE COLD   31

Five   SCIENCE AND CONSERVATION IN ANTARCTICA   45

Six   ANTARCTICA AND THE RACE TO SOLVE THE CLIMATE PUZZLE   57

Glossary   59

Further Reading and Resources   61

Index   64

CONTINENTS: WHERE WE STAND

The ground you stand on may seem solid and stable, but it's really moving all the time. How is that possible? Because all of the earth's continents, islands, oceans, and people ride on tectonic plates. These plates, which are huge slabs of the earth's crust, float on top of hot, melted rock below. One plate may carry a whole continent and a piece of an ocean. Another may carry only a few islands and some ocean. The plates shift, slide, and even bump together slowly as the molten rock below them flows.

Plate edges are where the action is, geologically speaking. That's where volcanoes erupt and earthquakes shake the land. Tectonic plates collide, gradually crumpling continents into folds that become mountains. Dry land, or ocean floor, can be made at these plate edges. Melted rock, spurting out of volcanoes or oozing out of cracks between plates, cools and solidifies. Dry land, or ocean floor, can also be destroyed here, as the edge of one tectonic plate slips underneath another. The moving, grinding plates create tremendous pressure and heat, which melts the rock, turning it into semisolid material.

Continents, the world's largest landmasses, the rock rafts where we live, ride on this shifting puzzle of tectonic plates. These continents are made of material that floated to the surface when much of the earth was hot and liquid long ago. The floating material then cooled and became solid. Two hundred and fifty million years ago there was only one continent, the supercontinent Pangaea, surrounded by one ocean, Panthalassa. But since then, the tectonic plates have moved, breaking apart the continents and rearranging them. Today there are seven continents: North America, South America, Europe, Asia, Africa, Australia, and Antarctica.

250 Million Years Ago

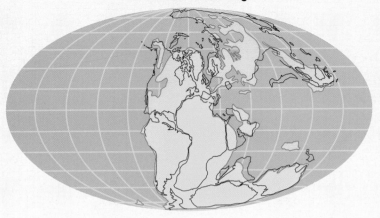

Two hundred and fifty million years ago there were only one continent and one ocean, as shown above. (Rough shapes the continents would eventually take are outlined in black.) The view below shows where the seven continents are today. These positions will continue to change slowly as tectonic plates shift.

Present Day

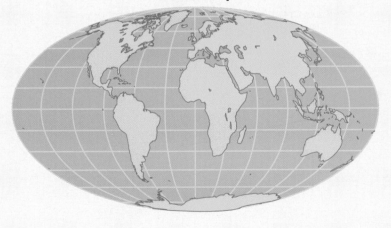

Each continent has its own unique character and conditions, shaped by its history and position on the earth. Europe, which is connected to Asia, has lots of coastline and moist ocean air. Australia, meanwhile, is influenced by its neighbor, Antarctica, which sends cool currents northward to its shores. North America and South America were once separated, but are now connected by Panama. Over the years, animals, from ancient camels to armadillos, have traveled the bridge in between these two continents.

A continent's landscape, geology, weather, and natural communities affect almost every human action taken on that continent, from planting a seed to waging a war. Rivers become the borders of countries. Soil determines what we can grow. Weather and climate affect our cultures—what we feel, how we dress, even how we celebrate.

Understanding continents can give us a deeper knowledge of the earth—its plants, animals, and people. It can help us see behind news headlines to appreciate the forces that shape world events. Such knowledge can be helpful, especially in a world that's constantly changing and shifting, down to the very earth beneath our feet.

*Not just your ordinary snow-covered mountain, Mt. Erebus is
Antarctica's only active volcano.*

ONE

GUIDE TO THE BOTTOM OF THE EARTH

At the South Pole lies a continent like no other. It's the coldest, highest, driest, iciest, windiest, least inhabited continent on the earth. Ninety-eight percent of it is covered by ice. Only two flowering plant species live on the entire continent. Its largest land animal is a wingless midge, an insect only $\frac{1}{2}$ inch (13 millimeters) long. That's not surprising, considering this continent—Antarctica—has the harshest living conditions of any.

Despite its frigid climate, Antarctica is a "hot spot" of sorts, because it has active volcanoes. Big Ben volcano and the Deception Island volcano have both erupted in the last fifty years. The 12,444-foot (3,794-meter) Erebus volcano on Ross Island erupted in 1991.

Antarctica is a hot spot in another sense too; it draws people and animals from other places on the earth. Arctic terns fly more than 12,500 miles (20,200 kilometers) from the Arctic to feed on Antarctica's bounty of fish in summer. Whales, such as blue whales, fin whales, and humpback whales, swim from their home territories to feed on krill, shrimp-like crustaceans that are abundant in the waters around Antarctica. These waters also teem with fish, seals, whales, and penguins and other seabirds. Thousands of tourists and scientists also visit Antarctica. They endure days of boat travel through some of the roughest seas on the earth to see and study Antarctica's penguins, its ancient ice, and its unearthly, frozen landscapes.

Antarctica is definitely the iciest continent. How much ice is there? Seventy percent of the earth's fresh water is frozen as Antarctic ice! A layer of ice 1.5 miles (2.4 kilometers) thick covers much of the continent. Ice cracks, melts, slides, and refreezes into strange shapes. Pieces of glaciers break off, forming floating chunks called icebergs. One iceberg, formed in October 1987, was almost as big as the state of Delaware!

Antarctic ice isn't amazing just for itself. It may hold the key to questions that affect everyone on the earth. Scientists drilling into the ice covering Antarctica have reached ice hundreds of thousands of years old. By studying this ice, and the air bubbles trapped in it, scientists can learn what the earth's air was like long ago. This information allows scientists to study how the earth's climate has changed over time and helps them predict how it may change in the future.

ABCs OF ANTARCTICA

Antarctica is the fifth-largest continent, covering 5.5 million square miles (14 million square kilometers). That's about half the size of Africa. Antarctica is located in the Southern Hemisphere, surrounding the South Pole. Lying offshore are scattered islands, such as Scott Island, the Balleny Islands, South Georgia Island, and the Sandwich Islands. They are considered part of the "subantarctic," the area around mainland Antarctica. The closest continent, South America, is 600 miles (1,000 kilometers) away. Surrounding Antarctica are the southernmost waters of the Pacific, Indian, and Atlantic oceans. Many geographers consider these waters to be a separate ocean: the Southern, or Antarctic, Ocean.

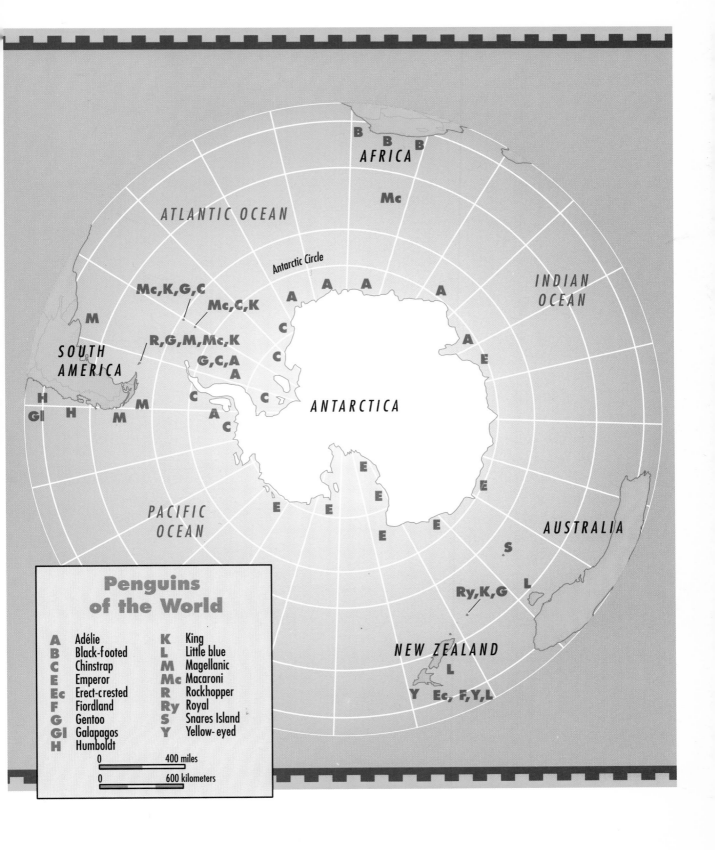

ATLANTIC OCEAN

B B
B

AFRICA

Mc

Antarctic Circle

A A A A

Mc,K,G,C

Mc,C,K

M

R,G,M,Mc,K

G,C,A

SOUTH
AMERICA

A

C

C

C

A

E

INDIAN
OCEAN

A

ANTARCTICA

H

Gl H H

M M

C

C

A
C

E

E

E

PACIFIC
OCEAN

E E

E

E

E

AUSTRALIA

S

L

Ry,K,G

NEW ZEALAND

L

Y Ec,F,Y,L

Penguins of the World

A	Adélie	**K**	King
B	Black-footed	**L**	Little blue
C	Chinstrap	**M**	Magellanic
E	Emperor	**Mc**	Macaroni
Ec	Erect-crested	**R**	Rockhopper
F	Fiordland	**Ry**	Royal
G	Gentoo	**S**	Snares Island
Gl	Galapagos	**Y**	Yellow-eyed
H	Humboldt		

0 ___ 400 miles

0 ___ 600 kilometers

Antarctica has two major sections: Greater Antarctica, also known as East Antarctica; and Lesser Antarctica, also known as West Antarctica. In between lie the Transantarctic Mountains, a range 3,000 miles (4,800 kilometers) long. Extending northward from Lesser Antarctica toward South America is the Antarctic Peninsula, an S-shaped sliver of land surrounded mostly by ocean. This peninsula is the warmest and most ice-free region of Antarctica.

No country owns Antarctica. In the past, seven countries had claims on Antarctica that were not recognized by all other countries. Now, the claims have been put aside and a system of treaties governs the continent.

WORLD RECORDS HELD BY ANTARCTICA

- World's coldest continent, with average winter temperatures of –74°F (–59°C) near the South Pole, and 6.8°F (–14°C) on the Antarctic Peninsula. Average summer temperatures are –26°F (–32°C) near the South Pole and 30°F (–1°C) on the Antarctic Peninsula
- World's windiest continent, with wind speeds of up to 200 miles (322 kilometers) per hour
- World's highest continent: average elevation 7,500 feet (2,300 meters)
- World's coldest recorded air temperature: –128.6°F (–89.2°C), on July 21, 1983, at Vostok

STATISTICS AND RECORDS WITHIN ANTARCTICA

- Area: 5.5 million square miles (14 million square kilometers)
- Highest peak: Vinson Massif 16,860 feet (5,139 meters)
- Average thickness of ice sheet: 1.5 miles (2.4 kilometers)
- Warmest temperature ever recorded: 59°F (15°C), Antarctic Peninsula

Drawn by breathtaking ice formations and other unique landscapes, tourists are arriving in Antarctica in ever greater numbers.

These icebergs in the Biscoe Islands, off the Antarctica Peninsula, dwarf the penguins in the foreground. Yet 80 to 90 percent of the icebergs' total weight lies beneath the sea.

TWO

ANTARCTIC ICE

Antarctica has mountains, hills, and valleys that no one will ever hike. That's because 98 percent of Antarctica is covered by a blanket of ice that hides these land features. This ice layer is 1.5 miles (2.4 kilometers) thick on average—and almost 3 miles (5 kilometers) deep in spots. Like an icy dome with a slightly flattened top, it forms a high, cold, windy plateau in the center of the continent, which slopes toward the coasts.

Antarctica's icy covering is so immense, it holds 70 percent of the earth's fresh water. This continental ice and the nearby sea ice affect not only Antarctica but worldwide ocean circulation. The ice forms strange shapes with complex structures that scientists study as part of their research on the continent.

HIGH AND LOW

Antarctica is considered the earth's highest continent—the one with the greatest average elevation. But most of the continent's actual bedrock lies below sea level, pressed down by the tremendous weight of the ice on top. Antarctica and its ice are so heavy that they slightly flatten the earth's shape near the South Pole!

ICE ON THE MOVE

Antarctic ice is always on the move. Ice slides slowly from the interior of Antarctica down toward the coasts. In fact, the Amundsen-Scott Station, where scientists live and

This glacier, like many others, has deep unseen crevasses.

work in buildings on the ice, is moving toward the South Pole at 33 feet (10 meters) a year! When ice reaches the coast, the edge of it floats, but part stays attached to the continent. These floating ice shelves form huge ice cliffs along Antarctica's coast.

When pieces break off from the ends of ice shelves, they become icebergs, floating out in the ocean. This iceberg-making process, called calving, has produced tens of thousands of icebergs around Antarctica. And some of those icebergs have been real whoppers! In 1987 Antarctic ice calved an iceberg named B-9. Before it broke up in 1989, B-9 measured 96 miles (155 kilometers) long and 22 miles (35 kilometers) wide—the size of Delaware. In 1995 scientists found an iceberg 656 feet (200 meters) thick and almost the size of Rhode Island. Because an iceberg floats, 90 percent of it is actually hidden below water. So an iceberg is much bigger than it looks from above water.

In 1987 several Soviet scientists tried to return to their summer research base in Antarctica. But their equipment and buildings were not where they had left them the summer before. These scientists spent weeks searching for their lost base. They finally found it on an iceberg that had broken off from the continent and floated far away!

THE CONTINENT THAT EXPANDS

Every winter, Antarctica seems to grow. From the air, it looks like the continent doubles in size. Actually, it's only the continent's bluish-white icy covering that expands outward. This occurs as the surface of the ocean freezes, forming sea ice. The expanding ring of ice advances outward at a rate of 2.6 miles (4.2 kilometers) per day. By the end of Antarctica's colder winters, the sea ice covers 7.7 million square miles (20 million square kilometers). In summer, the sea ice melts. Then, the next winter the sea ice forms again.

GREAT "ICESCAPES"

If you think frozen water comes in only three forms—snow, ice cubes, and popsicles—Antarctica will change your view. In this frigid environment, ice forms, builds up, and changes structure in a mind-boggling variety of ways.

GO, GLACIERS, GO!

Antarctica's icy covering is made up of glaciers, which are slow-moving, riverlike masses of ice; and ice sheets, which are glaciers that spread out over large areas. Glaciers and ice sheets start out as falling snow. When snow accumulates, the weight of the snow on top presses on the layers below, forming a dense type of ice called firn. The weight of the snow and the firn makes the glacier or ice sheet move slowly downhill. As the ice slides toward the sea, it divides in places into recognizable, riverlike glaciers. These glaciers do not flow smoothly. They move like slow-motion landslides. Some parts of the glacier move faster than others. This causes large cracks in the ice that can be hundreds of yards (meters) deep. These cracks, called crevasses, are hidden beneath the snow and can be hazardous for people walking, skiing, or riding snowmobiles.

FIRST GREASE, THEN PANCAKES

Sea ice has a complex structure, with many types of crystals. In stormy seas water freezes into frazil ice, which is slushy, with poorly formed ice crystals. In calmer waters, or after frazil has formed, the water freezes into grease ice, which gives the water a sheen like oil. In time, more freezing occurs on the moving ocean water, changing the frazil and grease

Here is a close-up view of some aptly named pancake ice in the Southern Ocean.

ice into pancake ice. Pancake ice looks like pancakes or lily pads scattered across the water's surface. Later in the winter, the "pancakes" grow bigger and stick together, forming larger pieces. Finally, these pieces form ice floes, large areas of frozen ice that are about 3 feet (almost a meter) thick.

BIG LAKE, BIG SECRETS

Antarctica has one of the world's largest, deepest freshwater lakes: Lake Vostok. However, this 1,764-foot- (510-meter-) deep lake isn't much good for sailing, swimming, or snorkeling. Not only is the water icy-cold, but it's hidden under 2.5 miles (4 kilometers) of ice! Scientists discovered the lake in the mid-1970s. In 1996, radar from a satellite showed that Lake Vostok is huge, covering 5,400 square miles (14,000 square kilometers)—more than two-thirds the size of Lake Ontario.

Does anything live in this hidden lake? Scientists would love to know, especially because the lake has been covered by ice for a half-million—maybe even a million—years. It has not been affected by modern pollutants such as PCBs (polychlorinated biphenyls), fallout from nuclear bombs, and radiation from reactor accidents. These pollutants circulate in the earth's atmosphere and settle out even in such remote places as Antarctica. Scientists expect to find nothing larger than microbes—microscopic organisms—in the lake. For now, they have agreed not to drill down through the ice into the lake until researchers can figure out how to study the lake without contaminating it.

ADD ICE AND STIR:
HOW ANTARCTICA STIRS THE OCEANS

The freezing of sea ice around Antarctica affects the entire earth. It helps mix the oceans and transfer heat from the Tropics—regions near the equator—to the poles. Here's how the heat transfer works: When water freezes into ice atop the ocean surrounding Antarctica, it leaves extremely salty, cold water below. This water, called brine, sinks because it is very dense. It seeps outward from Antarctica, deep in the ocean, and moves north toward the Tropics. Meanwhile, ocean water warmed in the sunny Tropics flows southward at the surface to replace the Antarctic water that sank and moved northward. This warm water, in turn, will eventually cool and sink, repeating the cycle over and over.

This cycle has an effect on the air because the temperature of water currents modifies air temperatures above. By carrying warm water to Antarctica, the current redistributes over 30 percent of the solar heat the earth receives. This flowing cycle makes air and water temperatures cooler in the Tropics and warmer in the Antarctic than they would be otherwise. Any disruption in the cycle caused by changes in Antarctica's temperature might drastically change the global climate—the earth's long-term weather conditions.

Scientists consider the Antarctic Convergence—the place where cold Antarctic water meets and sinks underneath warmer water coming from the Tropics—as the boundary of the Antarctic region. This area is also important to sea life, as you will read in Chapter 4.

The aurora australis—southern lights—create a dramatic night sky above the British Antarctic Survey's Halley Station.

THREE

ANTARCTICA: IT'S REALLY COOL!

Imagine spilling a cup of hot water that turns to ice before it hits the ground. Picture a day so cold that your sweat freezes inside your clothes. Think how you'd feel if the moisture in your breath coated your eyelashes with ice and caused your eyelids to freeze shut when you closed them. Explorers have experienced all these things and more in the coldest parts of Antarctica. Weather conditions there are so extreme that at times they can be dangerous. But the climate also creates breathtakingly beautiful skies and strange optical surprises.

DRIER THAN THE SAHARA

Even though Antarctica is icy, its air is extremely dry, especially in the center of the continent. The interior region is a polar desert, receiving less than 3 inches (7.5 centimeters) of precipitation a year. So how does Antarctica's icy covering, which is made of old snow, build up? The snow that does fall never melts. That's because the weather is below the freezing point of water all year, with average temperatures at the South Pole of –74°F (–59°C) in winter and –26°F (–32°C) in summer.

The coasts are warmer and snowier than the interior. But with an average winter temperature of 6.8°F (–14°C) and an average summer temperature of 30°F (–1°C), the weather is hardly toasty-warm.

WHY ANTARCTICA IS SO COLD

Each year, Antarctica receives almost as many hours of sunlight as places near the equator, such as Panama and northern Brazil. So why are they so warm and Antarctica so cold? The answer lies in the angle at which sunlight strikes the earth. Near the equator, the sun's rays hit Earth almost directly. But the sun's rays hit the poles at an angle, so the rays spread out. There's less sunlight—and heat energy—per square inch (centimeter) of land. What makes Antarctica even colder is that its ice reflects back into space as much as 90 percent of the sunlight it receives. So Antarctica doesn't absorb much heat, even on sunny days.

LONG DAYS, LONG NIGHTS

Days and nights near the earth's equator are about the same length all year long. But not in Antarctica. In January, during the Antarctic summer, days are long. At the peak of summer, the sun shines all day long! In July, during the Antarctic winter, the opposite occurs. Days become shorter, and on some days the sun does not rise above the horizon at all.

COLORFUL SHOW IN THE SKY

During winter nights in Antarctica, the sky sometimes lights up with incredible streaks of red, white, blue, and green. This light show is the aurora australis—the southern

ATLANTIC OCEAN

INDIAN OCEAN

SOUTH
AMERICA

Weddell
Sea

Bellingshausen
Sea

▲ Mt. Jackson

PENSICOLA MTS.

SOUTH POLAR
PLATEAU

AMERICAN
HIGHLANDS

South
Pole
+

▲ Mt. Vinson

ELLSWORTH MOUNTAINS

TRANSANTARCTIC MOUNTAINS

Amundsen
Sea

ROCKEFELLER
PLATEAU

▲ Mt. Sidney

Ross
Sea

PACIFIC OCEAN

▲ Mt. Erebus

INDIAN OCEAN

**Terrain Map
of Antarctica**

0   400 miles

0   600 kilometers

During a heavy gale near the South Georgia area, huge waves are churned up.

lights. A similar phenomenon visible in winter at the North Pole is called the aurora borealis—the northern lights. These natural "night lights" are caused by electrically charged particles emitted by the sun, which hit the earth's atmosphere.

Summer skies in Antarctica can be colorful, too—but not because of the southern lights. Arcs, circles, and lines of brilliant white light appear in the atmosphere. Straight rainbowlike bands of color reach up into the sky. These halos, sun pillars, fogbows, and other phenomena result from the interaction of sunlight or moonlight with ice crystals and supercooled water in the atmosphere.

REALLY GONE WITH THE WIND

Antarctica is the windiest continent, with winds blowing 50 miles (80 kilometers) per hour that sometimes last for weeks. Why is Antarctica so windy? Cold air, which is very dense and therefore heavy, slides down from the higher elevations in the center of the

THE HOLE IN THE OZONE

Each summer in Antarctica, scientists watch with concern for trouble in the skies. Scientific instruments carried by satellites, planes, and air balloons measure the thickness of the earth's ozone layer—a layer of ozone gas between about 12 and 21 miles (19 and 34 kilometers) above sea level in the atmosphere. Every spring since 1981, scientists have noticed a thinning of the ozone layer over Antarctica. This thin patch, at times as large as 22 million square miles (57 million square kilometers), and extending far beyond the borders of Antarctica, has been nicknamed the "ozone hole."

What difference does a hole in the ozone layer make? A lot. Ozone is the earth's armor against harmful radiation from the sun. Sunlight is made up of many wavelengths of light. Some wavelengths warm the earth and help plants grow. But the shortest-wavelength, highest-energy waves can be damaging to plants and animals. These rays, called ultraviolet rays, can cause skin cancer in people and damage mollusks, fish, and phytoplankton—small floating ocean plants. The ozone layer, like a layer of sunscreen lotion, helps protect the earth from much of the harmful ultraviolet radiation emitted by the sun.

Ozone loss is caused by chemicals such as chlorofluorocarbons (CFCs), which were once used in aerosol sprays, refrigerators, and Styrofoam. Countries have agreed to phase out CFCs and other ozone-destroying chemicals. But chemicals used in the past are still moving up into the atmosphere, thinning the ozone layer. (CFCs can last 60–100 years.) Because of the CFC ban, the amount of CFCs in the atmosphere is expected to begin declining in the early years of the twenty-first century.

The atmospheric ozone layer is thinning all over the earth. But the most thinning is over the polar regions, particularly over Antarctica, in spring. In the extreme cold of the dark Antarctic winter, chlorine atoms—released by CFCs—build up. In spring, the sun's ultraviolet rays energize the chlorine, setting in motion chemical reactions that destroy ozone. One chlorine atom can spark a sequence of reactions that destroys 100,000 ozone molecules. Scientists continue to monitor the thickness of the ozone layer, and study the effect of its decline on Antarctic animals.

continent toward the coasts, which are lower in elevation. This creates katabatic, or gravity, winds, which can gust at speeds of 200 miles (322 kilometers) per hour.

Cold katabatic winds meet warmer moist ocean air, and clouds, fog, and storms, including blizzards, may form. As a result, the coasts receive much more precipitation than the interior. As much as 30 inches (76 centimeters) of precipitation falls each year on the Antarctic Peninsula.

Due to gravity, katabatic winds come speeding off the
Antarctic icecap toward the coast.

STORMY SEAS

Beyond Antarctica's sea ice lie some of the stormiest seas on the earth. Westerly winds whip up waves. Cold air from over Antarctica clashes with warm air from the Tropics, creating swirling bands of storms called cyclones. Sailors call these stormy regions the Roaring Forties, the Furious Fifties, and the Screaming Sixties, referring to their latitudes. The cyclones occur especially between latitudes 60° and 65°. They circle the Southern Ocean, mixing masses of air, aiding in the global exchange of heat from the tropics to the poles. (This heat exchange was described in greater detail in Chapter 2.)

CLUES TO THE PAST

Has Antarctica always been a cold, icy, almost barren continent? Not according to paleontologists, scientists who study fossil plants and animals. In Antarctica they have discovered fossilized remnants of beech trees, ferns, crocodiles, and a flightless bird 6 feet

*Fossils of animals and plants, like this one, hold the key to
ancient life on Antarctica.*

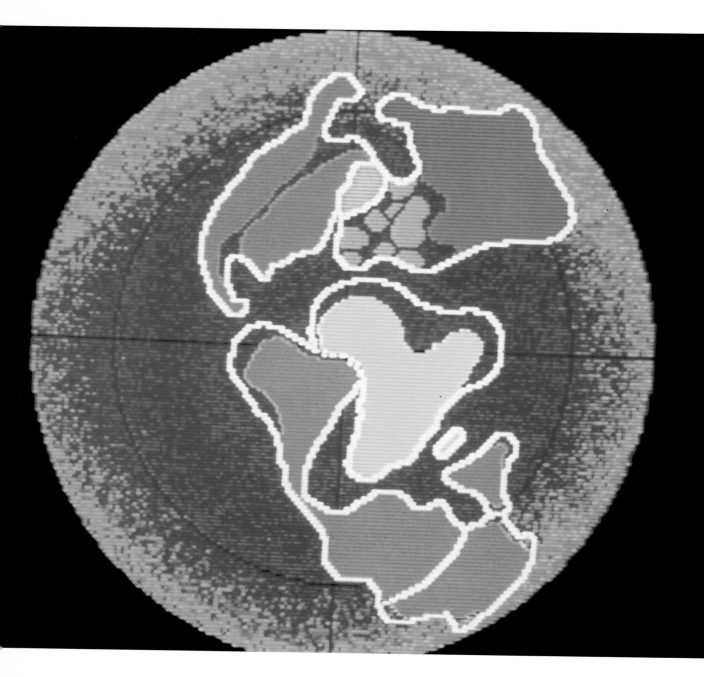

This computer image of the earth during the Cretaceous Period, 144–65 million years ago, shows Antarctica (in orange at bottom) surrounded by other continents. North America (green) and Eurasia (purple) are joined, as are South America and Australia (also in orange) and Africa (yellow).

(1.8 meters) tall. They have also found fossil bones belonging to small marsupials—pouched mammals—which may be the ancestors of marsupials that live in Australia today.

Scientists think that 70 million years ago Antarctica was covered by forests, not ice. At that time its present land area was surrounded by South America, Africa, Asia, Australia, and India. It was part of Gondwana, the southern half that broke off the great supercontinent of Pangaea. About 25 million years ago the forests died out, and Antarctica grew colder and colder as it moved south to its current location. Some scientists debate whether it has warmed then refrozen many times since then. Either way, standing on Antarctica's ice today, it's hard to imagine that forests once grew in this windy, icy place.

Adélie penguins gather in huge numbers to incubate their eggs.

FOUR

LIFE IN THE COLD

It's hard not to laugh at penguins. With their stout bodies, tuxedolike markings, and distinctive walk, they look like little waddling people. When they jump up out of the water, like corks popping out from bottles, they seem to be clowning around. When they flop on their bellies and slide along the ice, they seem too silly to be real. Yet the same physical features and behaviors we find laughable are actually adaptations that help penguins survive in Antarctica's cold seas. Like penguins, other Antarctic organisms have remarkable ways to survive, from blubbery bodies to natural antifreeze.

PLANTS IN STRANGE PLACES

With cold temperatures, mostly frozen water, almost no soil, and four months of little sunshine, Antarctica is far from an ideal place for land plants to grow. Yet plants do live there. In the rocky, dry, snowless valleys of central Antarctica, it's difficult to see the plants at first. But if you break apart a rock, you'll find layers of lichen, which live just under the surfaces of rocks, out of the cold and wind.

Lichens are a living partnership of algae and fungi. They live in tiny air spaces in sandstone, obtaining minerals from the rock. Air, sunlight, and water reach them through the rock's pores. Yeasts and cyanobacteria can live inside rocks, too.

Another surprising Antarctic plant appears as a red, green, or yellow stain in the snow. Such stains, found near the coasts, are actually algae. The algae use nutrients that

Lichens grow on the rocks of King George Island.

blow in on the wind, plus water and nutrients in melted snow. Melted snow is necessary, because plants can use only liquid water.

MOSSY MATS

Plants are easier to spot along Antarctica's coasts, particularly in warmer areas. Mosses and liverworts blanket rocks with fuzzy green carpets about 1 foot (30 centimeters) thick. Clumps of Antarctica's only flowering plants—Antarctic hair grass and Antarctic pearlwort—grow in sheltered spots. Nearby, flat patches of orange, red, and black lichens decorate rocks like colorful stickers. Some lichens grow very slowly, adding only 3/8–5/8 of an inch (10–16 millimeters) to their diameter in a century.

Growing conditions for plants are better along the coasts because of warmer weather, which brings rain and melting snow. Plant growth near bird colonies is often lush because bird droppings, called guano, fertilize the soil. Antarctic plants such as algae and mosses also live in cold lakes and along their shores. In all, Antarctica has approximately three hundred kinds of algae, eighty-five mosses, two hundred lichens, and twenty-five liverworts.

LAND ANIMALS: THEY'RE LITTLE SUCKERS

The largest land animal in Antarctica could fit on a penny. It's a wingless insect called a midge. Tiny wings would be useless in Antarctica, because strong winds make it hard to fly. Other land animals include mites and springtails, which are pinhead-size relatives of insects, called arthropods, that hop like fleas. Mites and springtails live in gravel or moss and eat plants or each other. Most of the other native animals are parasites—blood-sucking lice and fleas that hitchhike rides on seals and on penguins and other seabirds.

THE OCEAN GARDEN

Unlike the Antarctic continent, the surrounding ocean is teeming with wildlife, supporting whales, penguins, seals, fish, and krill. One reason for the bountiful wildlife is that cold, nutrient-rich water from deep in the ocean comes to the surface near Antarctica, and is stirred up by stormy, windy seas. At the surface, where there's sunlight, these nutrients can be used by phytoplankton, tiny floating ocean plants. With sunlight, water, and nutrients, phytoplankton carry out the process of photosynthesis, by which they make food. As the phytoplankton become more plentiful, ocean animals have a rich soup of food to eat. Even in winter, when the sea freezes over, phytoplankton can survive, living in and under the ice covering the sea.

*Krill, which are related to shrimp, are a major food source
for seabirds, seals, and whales.*

EAT 'EM UP: KRILL

Fish, seabirds, seals, and whales aren't the only ones pursuing krill these days. Fishing fleets from Japan, Ukraine, South Korea, the United Kingdom, and Poland catch about 80,000 tons of krill in a year. Krill aren't easy to eat. Their shells have to be removed right away, and their flesh spoils easily. Currently, only a small amount of krill is processed for use in fish products such as fish sticks and fish soup. Most of the krill harvested is used for feed for cattle, poultry, pigs, and fish on fish farms. Scientists are monitoring krill fisheries and negotiating limits on the catch.

KRILL FIT THE BILL

Where there are plants, there are usually plant eaters. In the ocean, tiny floating animals called zooplankton eat many of the phytoplankton. Shrimplike crustaceans called krill also eat phytoplankton, plus any zooplankton they scoop up along the way. Many different krill species of varying sizes live around Antarctica. The ones specifically called Antarctic krill are about 1½ inches (3.8 centimeters) long. Krill have six pairs of bristly limbs that form a basketlike structure. By squeezing water through this basket, they can filter phytoplankon and zooplankton out of the water. After a krill has eaten, you can see green phytoplankton inside its transparent, slightly pinkish body!

Krill are the major source of food for fish, many seabirds, some seals, and some whales. Fortunately, they are numerous. At times so many swim close together that they make the water look pink. Swarms of krill can stretch for several miles (kilometers). But people rarely see them because krill typically remain deep in the water during the day, rising to the surface only at night.

"SUPERCOOL" FISH

When it comes to being cool, no animal can beat a group of Antarctic fish called Notothenioids. Their blood is colder than 32°F (0°C), the temperature at which pure water freezes. (Talk about being cold-blooded!) Antifreeze molecules in their bodies keep their blood and body fluids from forming ice crystals, which could otherwise rupture their cells. Speaking of blood, one Notothenioid species, called the ice fish, has blood that's almost colorless. This fish has no hemoglobin, the red molecules that help the

An emperor penguin chick rests on the feet of its parent,
safe and warm up off the ice and snow.

blood in most animals to carry oxygen. Instead, an ice fish has a fast-beating heart and large blood vessels, which enable the small amount of oxygen in its blood to get to its cells, even without hemoglobin. Notothenioids and other Antarctic fishes tend to grow slowly and live a long time.

PENGUINS ON PARADE

Penguins are not land animals. They are seabirds. They feed on krill, squid, and fish in the ocean, going ashore only to rest, lay eggs, and raise their young. Penguins are superbly adapted for life in cold seas. Their bodies contain lots of blubber, a thick fat that helps them stay warm in cold water. Long, overlapping feathers with downy feathers underneath also help them keep warm. Penguins cannot survive in warm water for very long; they overheat. No wonder all the world's penguins live in the cold waters of the Southern Hemisphere. Adélie, chinstrap, emperor, gentoo, king, macaroni, and rockhopper penguins live in or near Antarctica.

All penguin species are primarily black and white. The penguin's "tuxedo" coloring helps it fit in—not at a formal party but with the colors of the ocean. When seen from above, a penguin's dark back matches the dark sea bottom. When seen from below, a penguin's white underside matches the lighter sky or ice above. This camouflage helps penguins hide from both predators and prey, increasing their success both in hunting and in overall survival.

SEE PENGUINS SWIM

A penguin's body is streamlined, so it can move swiftly through water with minimal energy. Unlike the wings of other birds, a penguin's "wings" are smooth, more like paddles—perfect for pushing through the sea. At times, penguins almost seem to be flying underwater as they flap their paddles and glide. They also "porpoise"—leap out of the water, as porpoises do, while traveling at high speeds. Scientists believe this behavior may save penguins and porpoises energy. Air offers less resistance to forward motion than water does. (Just think how much easier it is to walk forward through air than through deep water in a swimming pool.) Jumping out of water, even for a moment, lets penguins travel farther and faster. Penguins are also superb divers. When hunting for food, king penguins can dive more than 800 feet (244 meters) deep.

Although graceful underwater, penguins travel awkwardly on land. With short legs set far back on their bodies, penguins can only waddle or hop. (That's where rockhopper penguins got their name.) At times, it's faster and more efficient for penguins to flop on their bellies and slide across the ice to get where they are going.

TIMES OF SLAUGHTER

The wealth of marine life in the Southern Ocean has attracted people to Antarctica for hundreds of years. In the late 1760s and early 1770s, Captain Cook sailed in the Southern Ocean and wrote letters and journals describing the huge numbers of seals, penguins, and whales he saw. Soon after, fleets of ships from England and America sailed to the Southern Ocean and slaughtered hundreds of thousands of fur and elephant seals. The seal hides were used to make clothes and felt hats; their blubber was boiled down for oil. Within a century, fur seals were practically wiped out, and there were too few elephant seals for hunters to bother traveling to Antarctica.

Penguins, however, were still plentiful. Penguin eggs were collected by the barrel. Sailors ate the penguin eggs and meat. In the late 1800s, penguin skins and feathers were also used to decorate women's hats and clothes. In the same period, millions of penguins were clubbed to death, then boiled down for oil. The oil was used for making soap, tanning leather, and burning in lamps. Whaling in the Antarctic began in 1904 and continued into the 1970s, when it was banned except for scientific uses. Whales were harvested for meat, blubber, oil, and ambergris, a waxy substance used in perfume.

PENGUIN PARENTS YOU WON'T BELIEVE

In the frigid darkness of Antarctica's winter, the world's largest penguins huddle together to stay warm. These 3.5-foot- (1.2-meter-) tall emperor penguins, all males, have not eaten for weeks. They shuffle slowly, taking turns being on the chilly outer edge of the group, before shuffling back toward the center. Emperor penguins are the only warmblooded animals that stay on the continent in winter. Hidden under a fold of feather and skin, each male holds a treasure: a softball-size egg, which sits balanced on his toes.

After several weeks, these eggs hatch into chicks. Each father, though starved for food, feeds his chicks with a special oil secreted in his throat. The chick grows downy and fat while nestled under a fold of feathers and skin, balanced on its father's toes. It must stay off the ice or it will die within two minutes because of the cold.

By the time the females return from the sea, where they have been fattening up on fish, the males have not eaten in two months. Once larger than the females, the males have lost 40 percent of their body weight and are now smaller than their partners. After a head-bobbing greeting, some calls, and some shuffling around, the male penguin transfers the chick to the female's feet. Now the females take over feeding the chicks. It's time for the males to go to sea. Sometimes the males have to trek as much as 60 miles (nearly 100 kilometers) overland to reach the sea. There they can catch fish and fatten up, before returning to help raise their young.

Once the chicks have grown and have lots of feathers, they can climb off their parent's feet. The chicks huddle together in a group called a crèche, a sort of nursery. Meanwhile, their parents hunt for food in the sea. When the parents return, the chick and its parents can find and recognize each other by voice. In time, the emperor penguin chicks will jump into the cold sea and learn to feed and take care of themselves.

SKUAS AND OTHER SEABIRDS

Close to penguin colonies, you're likely to find skuas—large, seagull-like birds. Skuas are opportunists. They swoop in and grab and eat any penguin egg or chick that is not closely guarded by a parent. Skuas also pester other birds until the birds drop their fish or pick up food spilled when a penguin feeds its chick. Skuas raise their own chicks at the same time penguins are nesting, so they can feed them food gathered at penguin colonies.

Other seabirds that live in and around Antarctica include albatrosses, petrels, fulmars, terns, and gulls. These birds feed on squid, krill, and fish, which are plentiful in the Southern Ocean.

SEALS: THE DIVING CHAMPIONS

Like penguins, most seals have thick, slick, blubbery, torpedo-shaped bodies that help them stay warm and swim fast. Six seal species inhabit the Southern Ocean: crabeater, elephant, fur, Weddell, leopard, and Ross seals. Like whales, seals must swim to the surface periodically for air. Weddell seals gnaw holes in sea ice so they can poke their noses up and take breaths. Seals are also terrific divers. Weddell seals can stay underwater for more than an hour. They may dive to 2,000 feet (600 meters) while pursuing squid and fish. During dives, their heart rate and metabolism slow, reducing their need for oxygen. Antarctic seals vary in size, physical features, and behavior. Male elephant seals are huge: nearly 15 feet (4.5 meters) long and weighing as much as 4 tons! In fact, southern elephant seals are the largest seals in the world. Fur seals are only 6.5 feet (2 meters) long and weigh 200–250 pounds (90–115 kilograms). Elephant seals keep warm with lots of blubber. Fur seals have less blubber, but their thick fur keeps them warm. Crabeater

Two bull elephant seals play-fight in the South Orkney Islands.

seals, the most numerous, don't eat crabs at all; they dine on krill. They gulp a mouthful of krill-filled water, then spit out the water, holding in the krill with their teeth. Leopard seals, which grow as long as 12 feet (3.7 meters), are named for their spots. Leopard seals eat not only krill but also penguins and young crabeater seals.

WHO'S DINING AT THE ANTARCTIC BUFFET

What animal is 100 feet (30 meters) long, has a heart the size of a small car, and can eat 8 tons (7 tonnes) of krill in a day? A blue whale. Blue whales are the largest animals ever to live on Earth. These huge marine mammals are just one of the many whale species that visit Antarctica in summer. During that season, whales feast on krill and fish, building up blubber that helps sustain them in other parts of the year when food is less plentiful, and when females are pregnant and nursing.

Most of the visiting whale species—blue, fin, sei, minke, right, and humpback—are baleen whales. These whales have a bristled, comblike fringe in their mouth called baleen that helps strain phytoplankton, krill, and small fish out of seawater. Sperm whales and other toothed whales hunt larger prey such as squid. Killer whales, which are large dolphins, swim in family groups and hunt together, eating penguins, seals, and fish.

A WHALE OF A CONNECTION

Whales are the biggest animals on Earth. But when in Antarctica, they depend on one of the shortest, simplest food chains in nature. Blue whales eat krill, which, in turn, eat phytoplankton. Without phytoplankton or krill, the blue whales would die.

What would happen if you took whales out of the food chain? In a way, that occurred in the late-nineteenth and early-twentieth centuries. Many kinds of whales were hunted and killed worldwide, drastically decreasing their populations.

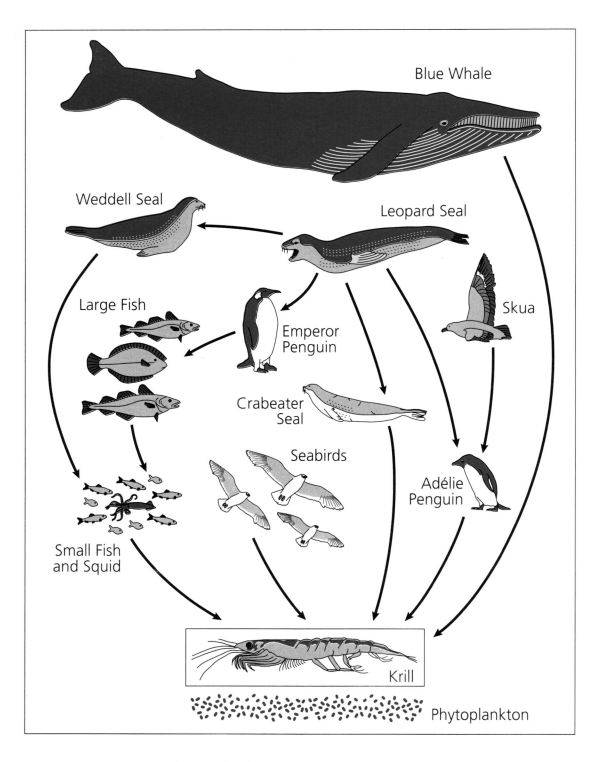

A complicated food web in the seas around Antarctica?
Not for the blue whale, which eats krill, which eat phytoplankton.

With so many whales gone, were there more krill for other krill eaters? That may be the case. In the twentieth century, populations of crabeater seals, which eat krill, and penguins, which eat both krill and krill-eating fish, have boomed. Scientists suspect, but cannot prove, that these populations benefited from the whales' decline. It is impossible to know for sure because populations do change naturally. Now the question is how harvesting by humans of krill and other fish from the Southern Ocean will affect the wildlife of Antarctica.

Pointy Hill rises behind McMurdo Station's Ice Pier.

FIVE

SCIENCE AND CONSERVATION IN ANTARCTICA

Antarctica is the "last frontier": the least polluted, least inhabited, wildest, most untouched continent on the earth. This reservoir of clean air and clean water holds scientific secrets that are difficult to study anywhere else. At present, Antarctica is mainly a site for scientific study, with more than forty permanent research sites. But in recent years people with other interests in Antarctica have been visiting in larger numbers.

Each year thousands of tourists arrive, hoping to see penguins, seals, whales, and spectacular scenery. Sports enthusiasts seek thrills skiing, hiking, skydiving, and climbing in the extreme conditions on the continent. Offshore, fishing fleets have been harvesting greater and greater amounts of fish and krill. Some countries have also been investigating whether Antarctica, despite its icy covering, might contain enough oil, coal, and valuable minerals to make mining worthwhile someday.

Despite its vast land and ocean area, Antarctica is unlikely to accommodate all these competing uses in the future. Fortunately, recent international agreements help countries work together to ensure a peaceful, unpolluted Antarctica for years to come.

ANTARCTIC RESEARCH

Scientists conduct research in Antarctica for many reasons. The main reason is that Antarctica holds a record of life that stretches back to prehistoric times. This record is in Antarctica's ice, which is formed from snow that has fallen over hundreds of millen-

45

nia. By drilling down into the ice sheet, scientists can pull up samples of ice from hundreds of thousands of years ago.

To take a sample, scientists lower a 3-inch- (7.6-centimeter-) diameter pipe with a heated end into the ice. The heated end melts the ice, enabling the pipe to push deeper and cut a cylindrical sample called a core. Scientists pull up the core and study it in a cold laboratory, where the temperatures are kept below freezing so the core won't melt.

Dust, pollen grains, and air bubbles have been found in ice cores. By analyzing the chemistry of the ice cores, scientists can find out about the ancient earth. Volcanic ash indicates a volcanic eruption. Pollen grains indicate what plants grew in Antarctica or on other continents from which the pollen might have blown in. Ice cores may even contain radioactive particles released during nuclear tests conducted by the United States in the 1950s.

Climatologists, scientists who study the earth's climate, also measure the amount of carbon dioxide and oxygen found in air bubbles trapped in ancient ice. They have learned that the amounts of carbon dioxide and methane (a compound of carbon and hydrogen) in the earth's atmosphere have been increasing over time. Both of these are greenhouse gases—they trap heat from sunlight in the earth's atmosphere the way greenhouse glass does. Many scientists are concerned that the buildup of greenhouse gases is causing global warming, an overall increase in the earth's temperature. By studying ice cores, scientists can see how the earth's climate has changed over time. This may help them understand how it is changing today and may change in the future.

BE A METEORITE HUNTER

Slip on five layers of clothing, a pair of goggles, a warm hat and hood, and jump on a snowmobile. You're ready for meteorite hunting in Antarctica. You might find a rock from Mars or some other planet, or perhaps from an asteroid. Each year, meteorites—rocks from outer space—land all over Earth. But the best place to find them is in Antarctica.

Antarctica's ice sheet is like a giant freezer full of meteorites that have fallen over a period of thousands of years. As the ice sheet moves and is eroded by the wind, the meteorites are revealed. Because they are dark in color, they are relatively easy to see against the blue ice and white snow. Meteorites vary in size; they can be as small as golf balls or as big as footballs.

Riding snowmobiles, scientists scan the ice surface, searching for meteorites. When they find one, they carefully record the location. They use a global positioning device, a small, hand-held instrument that tells them their position by receiving signals from satellites orbiting Earth.

Roberta Score, a scientist working for ANSMET (Antarctic Search for Meteorites), found a meteorite from Mars in 1984. It has structures that some scientists believe could be fossils, which may indicate the planet once had life.

This geologist, who has traveled by snowmobile to hunt for meteorites, stoops to examine one of his finds.

Scientists also study meteorites for clues about how the solar system developed. Many meteorites are 4.5 billion years old. Scientists find as many as one thousand meteorites in a summer. Finding each one brings new surprises and the chance to learn more about the universe.

ANTARCTICA: NOT BLINDED BY THE LIGHT

When people go outdoors at night to look at the stars, they turn off flashlights and car headlights and wait several minutes for their eyes to adjust to the darkness. Gradually, the stars seem brighter and brighter, and the stargazers can see more and more stars.

The stars aren't really getting brighter or more numerous. Human eyes and scientific instruments just see it that way. They can best detect the dim light of stars, comets, and planets when other strong lights are not around. Even miles away from a city, you can see the haze of light in the atmosphere from the city's streetlamps, signs, searchlights, house lights, and car headlights. This haze, called light pollution, interferes with the research done by astronomers, scientists who study stars, planets, and other features of outer space. For an astronomer, looking at stars from a light-filled city is like your trying to hear a soft-speaking person in a noisy crowd.

Antarctica, with artificial lighting only at research bases, is one of the best places to

These rusting barrels filled with chemicals are just one form of pollution that may threaten Antarctica's ecosystem.

find "real" darkness. Air near the South Pole contains very little water vapor and pollution, enabling astronomers to see stars particularly clearly. There are plans to build several observatories in Antarctica to better study outer space.

ALL SORTS OF SCIENCE

Observing stars, hunting meteorites, and analyzing ice aren't the only kinds of research done in Antarctica. Dr. Kathy Conlan, of the Canadian Museum of Nature, has been studying how human sewage pumped into the ocean near McMurdo Station, a scientific research base, affects animals and plants on the ocean floor. Conlan's study requires SCUBA diving under Antarctic ice to observe the shrimps, crabs, sea stars, and plankton. Other Antarctic scientists track animals by sound, recording calls of killer whales. Some attach radio transmitters to penguins or seals, then follow their movements to find out how deep they dive. These studies and others help scientists understand how animals can survive in the harsh conditions of Antarctica, and how the presence of humans is beginning to affect the Antarctic ecosystem.

ANTARCTIC ISSUES

In the cold, dry air of Antarctica, it takes a long time for material to rot and decay. You can still see cans of food and piles of garbage left by Antarctic explorers in the early years of the twentieth century. Even the carcasses of sled dogs are slightly mummified, their skin and collars still intact. Like a freezer, Antarctica preserves what's left there. Unfortunately, over the years, that's included garbage, untreated sewage, old batteries, oil drums, rusted trucks, aluminum cans, glass bottles, and toxic waste left by scientists and explorers near their research sites. Are these pollutants harming the plants and animals of Antarctica? Scientists recently found that some Antarctic penguins have diseases that most likely came from bacteria and viruses in sewage and garbage that was dumped on the continent or in nearby waters.

Today, explorers and research stations are working to clean up these messes and prevent them in the future. Some expeditions ship out all the waste they generate, including sewage. But accidents can still happen. In 1989, an Argentine navy ship ran aground on rocks just off the coast of Antarctica. The ship spilled 170,000 gallons (643,500 liters) of diesel oil, which coated the water and beaches, and killed hundreds of birds.

HOW MANY IS TOO MANY?

More than seven thousand tourists visited Antarctica during the 1996–1997 tourist season. That number is expected to double within five years. Handling garbage and sewage from an increasing tourist population is a challenge. But environmentalists and tour

In St. Andrews Bay, tourists are still greatly outnumbered by penguins!

operators are working on this problem, and are particularly trying to make sure that tourists do not disturb penguin and seal colonies.

WHAT'S THE CATCH?

Overfishing, the harvest of too many fish and shellfish, is a growing threat to Antarctica's marine wildlife. The numbers of fish such as Atlantic cod and ice fish have decreased so much that fishing fleets have turned to harvesting other fish. In 1997 at least seventy vessels pursued Patagonian toothfish, which are 6½ feet (2 meters) long and weigh up to 65 pounds (30 kilograms). Limits have been set on how many Patagonian toothfish can be caught. But in 1997 illegal fishing by unlicensed boats caught about four times the set limit. Patagonian toothfish live deep in the ocean and do not lay eggs until they are eight years old. So even if fishing is stopped, it may take a long time for their population to build up again. Overfishing of krill, squid, and other species is also of concern.

Another problem is that fishing boats don't catch just fish. They also accidentally capture seabirds that are attracted to the bait and get caught on hooks and in lines. Albatrosses and petrels are particularly at risk. An estimated 45,000 to 145,000 seabirds are killed in a year by illegal fishing boats near Antarctica. Conservationists have asked fishing fleets to fish only during special seasons, set by international agreement.

NOT SO REMOTE, AFTER ALL

Antarctic seabirds, such as penguins, petrels, and fulmars, live thousands of miles from factories and waste incinerators. Yet their bodies still contain deadly pollutants. In 1997 a Dutch scientist found that the natural oil Antarctic birds use to preen their feathers contains startlingly large amounts of hexachlorobenzene (HCB), a toxic air pollutant released by industrial incinerators. The scientist believes HCB may be one of many chemical vapors that rises up into the atmosphere over the earth's warm parts. These chemicals travel the globe in the upper atmosphere. At the poles, the vapors cool, condense, and fall to earth, where they contaminate birds and other animals.

IS THERE GOLD IN ANTARCTICA?

Antarctica was once connected to South America, which has a wealth of minerals. The Transantarctic mountains are actually an extension of the Andes. Antarctica's geology indicates that considerable amounts of gold, silver, zinc, copper, and lead may lie below the ice sheet. Coal and oil may be under there, too. Getting to these materials, however,

Some pollution is a side effect of scientific studies. Each year, scientists in Antarctica release thousands of scientific balloons into the atmosphere, carrying scientific instruments. Unlike planes, balloons do not pollute the Antarctic air with exhaust. But when the balloons come down, they are not retrieved, so they become garbage on land or in the sea. Balloons are dangerous to whales and other wildlife, which may mistake them for food and choke on them.

would be very difficult. It is unlikely that anyone will start mining or oil drilling in Antarctica until the earth's more accessible, more easily harvested supplies are depleted.

Nevertheless, in the 1970s, when oil-rich Middle Eastern nations cut back on their production and oil became scarce, many countries became interested in mining in Antarctica. They worked for years to formulate an international agreement called the Convention on the Regulation of Antarctic Mineral Resource Activities, which would have allowed limited mining in Antarctica. However, environmentalists worldwide objected to any kind of mineral exploitation of Antarctica. So Australia and France eventually withdrew their support of the agreement, calling instead for the establishment of Antarctica as a world park. The mining agreement was never signed. Countries negotiated instead to create the Protocol on Environmental Protection, which protects Antarctica and prevents mining.

CONSERVATION AND THE FUTURE OF ANTARCTICA

WHO OWNS ANTARCTICA?

Since its discovery, Antarctica has belonged to no single nation. In the early 1900s seven nations—Argentina, Australia, Chile, France, New Zealand, Norway, and the United Kingdom (Great Britain)—claimed pie-shaped portions of Antarctica. But these claims were never recognized worldwide.

During the International Geophysical Year of 1957–1958, a celebration of scientific research, researchers from sixty-seven nations studied Antarctica. That year, scientists and diplomats created the Antarctic Treaty, an international agreement to safeguard the continent for scientific research. This treaty, which went into force in 1961, put on hold claims on Antarctica by individual countries indefinitely. Antarctica was declared a site

TREATIES THAT GOVERN ANTARCTICA

Today, Antarctica is governed by the Antarctic Treaty System, a network of agreements among forty-three nations. These agreements include:

- The Antarctic Treaty of 1961
  Antarctica shall be used for peaceful purposes; no single country owns it; nuclear weapons, nuclear dumping, and military operations, except related to scientific studies, are banned.

- Agreed Measures on the Conservation of Antarctic Flora and Fauna, 1966
  Prohibits killing, capturing, or interfering with native mammals or birds without a permit; minimizes water pollution; establishes special protected areas.

- Convention on the Conservation of Antarctic Seals, 1978
  Prohibits killing or capturing fur seals, elephant seals, and Ross seals in Antarctica. Limits the number of crabeater seals, leopard seals, and Weddell seals that can be harvested.

- Convention on the Conservation of Antarctic Marine Living Resources, 1982
  Regulates fishing in the Southern Ocean surrounding Antarctica.

- Protocol on Environmental Protection to the Antarctic Treaty, 1998
  Prohibits mineral exploitation for fifty years; requires environmental assessment of activities in Antarctica.

for international scientific research and information exchange. Twelve nations signed the treaty. Since that time, the continent has been controlled entirely through international agreements.

VICTORY FOR ANTARCTIC PROTECTION

December 15, 1997, was a victorious day for people working to keep Antarctica a natural wilderness. On that day, Japan ratified the Antarctic Environmental Protocol, an international agreement that strengthened the Antarctic Treaty established thirty-six years before. (The protocol had been signed in 1991, but could not take effect until it was ratified—approved by the legislatures—in all twenty-six nations with voting rights.)

The protocol then took effect in January 1998. The protocol bans mining in Antarctica for at least fifty years and declares the continent and surrounding seas "a natural reserve devoted to peace and science."

The protocol requires that the environmental impact of any activity on the continent be studied and assessed before that activity can take place. The protocol regulates tourism, waste disposal, and dumping of garbage. It also protects Antarctic land plants, bird rookeries, and seal colonies. Under the protocol, certain scientific, historic, or wilderness areas can be given further protection and entered only with a permit.

Just as it has taken many years of hard work to put together the protocol, enforcing it will require the cooperation of many nations for years to come. If successful, this protocol will help countries work together to safeguard Antarctica more effectively in the future.

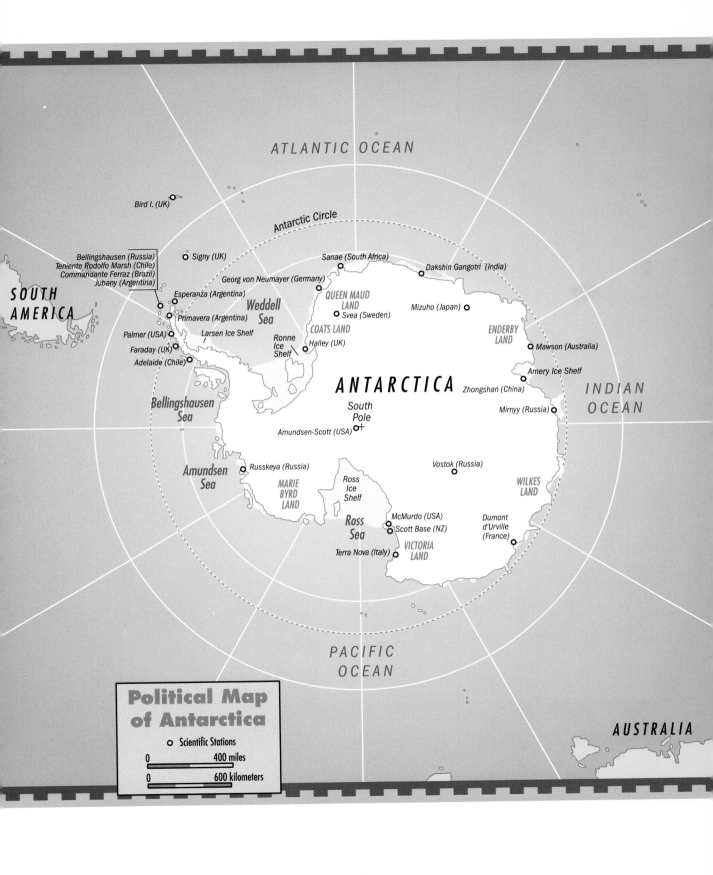

ATLANTIC OCEAN

Bird I. (UK)

Antarctic Circle

Bellingshausen (Russia)
Teniente Rodolfo Marsh (Chile)
Commandante Ferraz (Brazil)
Jubany (Argentina)

Signy (UK)

Sanae (South Africa)

Dakshin Gangotri (India)

Georg von Neumayer (Germany)

Esperanza (Argentina)

QUEEN MAUD
LAND

Mizuho (Japan)

SOUTH
AMERICA

Weddell
Sea

Svea (Sweden)

ENDERBY
LAND

Primavera (Argentina)

COATS LAND

Palmer (USA)

Larsen Ice Shelf

Ronne
Ice
Shelf

Halley (UK)

Mawson (Australia)

Faraday (UK)

Amery Ice Shelf

Adelaide (Chile)

ANTARCTICA

INDIAN
OCEAN

Bellingshausen
Sea

South
Pole

Zhongshan (China)

Mirnyy (Russia)

Amundsen-Scott (USA)

Amundsen
Sea

Russkeya (Russia)

Vostok (Russia)

WILKES
LAND

MARIE
BYRD
LAND

Ross Ice
Shelf

Ross
Sea

McMurdo (USA)

Scott Base (NZ)

Dumont
d'Urville
(France)

Terra Nova (Italy)

VICTORIA
LAND

PACIFIC
OCEAN

Political Map
of Antarctica

○ Scientific Stations

0   400 miles

0   600 kilometers

AUSTRALIA

Sunsets such as this one along the Graham Coast of the Antarctic Peninsula set off icebergs in dramatic relief.

SIX

ANTARCTICA AND THE RACE TO SOLVE THE CLIMATE PUZZLE

When you wake up every morning, do you think about global climate? Floods? Droughts? Famines? Animal die-offs? Record crop surpluses? Shrinking glaciers? Rising sea levels? Blizzards? All these events, covered in news headlines worldwide, are linked to the earth's weather and climate—its long-term weather conditions.

Scientists have become concerned because the earth as a whole is getting warmer. The global air temperature rose by 0.9°F (0.5°C) in the second half of the twentieth century. Nobody is sure how global warming will affect the earth in the future.

Global warming isn't like turning up the heat in a room. It is not felt evenly all over the earth. Some areas may actually become cooler. Climate patterns will likely shift, making some areas warmer or cooler, drier or wetter, than usual. Predicting how global warming will affect any given place is difficult because scientists must consider the interactions between such factors as landmasses, bodies of water, ocean currents, atmospheric winds, ocean chemistry, the strength of the sun's energy output, the behavior of organisms, and the burning of tropical forests.

So far, climate change has been most noticeable at the poles. On the Antarctic Peninsula, average yearly air temperatures have risen 5°F (2.3°C) in the second half of the twentieth century. The warmer climate has led to heavier snowfall, because warmer air holds more moisture. One result of this is fewer bare rocky areas, which are the ideal nesting sites for Adélie penguins. Perhaps in part because of the fewer sites, the number of breeding pairs of Adélies decreased from 15,200 in 1975 to 9,200 in 1997.

Another indication of a warmer world is a decrease in Antarctica's sea ice, which usually freezes outward from the continent in March or April. Very cold winters, when the sea ice freezes over a tremendous area, have become rarer since the mid-twentieth century.

The change in the amount of sea ice could greatly affect the food web of the entire Southern Ocean. That is because algae thrive on the underside of the sea ice in winter. Less sea ice means fewer algae. Fewer algae means fewer krill. Fewer krill means penguins, seals, and whales could go hungry. So far, scientists are not sure how the decrease in sea ice has affected ocean animals. But the amount of krill near the Antarctic Peninsula has decreased substantially since the early 1980s.

Is the population decline of Adélies and krill due to global warming and sea-ice decline? It's too early to say. There could be other factors.

Another result of warmer air temperatures is that ice shelves around Antarctica have become unstable. Large icebergs have broken off, and large cracks have been seen in the ice shelves. But some iceberg formation and some cracks are normal. So are these recent events "unusual"? To find out, scientists are doing research. One scientist is even studying old whaling records to find descriptions of how far the sea ice extended decades ago!

For now, scientists are left with questions and more questions. If Antarctica's ice is melting, how will it affect the rest of the earth? Will sea levels rise substantially? Will ocean circulation change? Like a ripple in a pond, even a small change in Antarctica could be felt all over the earth. That is one more reason scientists feel an urgent need to unravel Antarctica's scientific mysteries.

GLOSSARY

Antarctic Convergence—a zone surrounding Antarctica where cold water from the south meets and sinks below warmer water from the Tropics. It is considered the border of the antarctic region.

Antarctic Treaty System—a set of international agreements governing activities on the continent of Antarctica and in surrounding waters

aurora australis—glowing bands of red, green, and white light occasionally visible in southern skies at night, caused by charged particles from the sun interacting with earth's atmosphere

baleen—a comblike structure in the mouths of some whale species that helps whales strain small food particles out of seawater

brine—very salty water

calving—the process by which icebergs break off from glaciers

chlorofluorocarbons—a group of compounds once used as refrigerants, in aerosol cans, and in the production of Styrofoam. These compounds lead to the breakdown of the ozone layer, so their use is being phased out.

climatologist—a scientist who studies long-term weather conditions

firn—snow that has been compacted to form glacial ice

glacier—a large mass of slow-moving ice

59

global warming—the overall rise in the earth's air temperature. Scientists expect this rise in temperature will be felt unevenly on earth, causing some areas to become warmer and others cooler. Global warming may be occurring partly because of industrial pollution that has led to a buildup of greenhouse gases around the earth.

greenhouse gases—gases that trap heat from sunlight in the earth's atmosphere, the way greenhouse glass does

iceberg—a floating block of ice produced by calving

ice sheet—a glacier that spreads out over a large area

ice shelf—a floating sheet of ice that is connected on one end to a glacier

katabatic wind—a wind created by a cold mass of air sliding down an incline

krill—small ocean-dwelling crustaceans important to the Antarctic food chain

meteorite—a piece of matter from outer space that enters the earth's atmosphere and falls, intact, to the ground. (Pieces that burn up in the atmosphere and never make it to the ground are called meteors.)

ozone layer—a layer of ozone gas, high up in the mesosphere and stratosphere, that protects the earth from harmful ultraviolet radiation from the sun

phytoplankton—tiny, often microscopic, plants that float in the ocean

Southern Ocean—the ocean, also called the Antarctic Ocean, that surrounds the continent of Antarctica

zooplankton—tiny animals that travel through the ocean primarily by floating along with the currents

FURTHER READING

(Books marked with an asterisk are geared for young readers.)

BOOKS

* Billings, Henry. *Antarctica*. Chicago: Children's Press, 1994.
* Flegg, Jim. *Poles Apart: The Natural Worlds of the Arctic and Antarctic*. London: Pelham Books, 1990.
* Johnson, Rebecca. *Braving the Frozen Frontier: Women Working in Antarctica*. Minneapolis: Lerner, 1996.
* ———. *Science on the Ice: An Antarctic Journal*. Minneapolis: Lerner, 1995.

May, John. *The Greenpeace Book of Antarctica*. New York: Doubleday, 1989.
* McMillan, Bruce. *Life Along the Antarctic Peninsula*. New York: Houghton Mifflin, 1995.

Moss, Sanford. *Natural History of the Antarctic Peninsula*. New York: Columbia University Press, 1988.
* Pringle, Laurence P. *Antarctica: Our Last Unspoiled Continent*. New York: Simon & Schuster, 1992.

Soper, Tony. *Antarctica: A Guide to the Wildlife*. Old Saybrook, CT: Globe Pequot Press, 1994.
* Winckler, Suzanne, and Mary M. Rodgers. *Our Endangered Planet: Antarctica*. Minneapolis: Lerner, 1992.
* Woods, Michael. *Science on the Ice: Research in the Antarctic*. Brookfield, CT: Millbrook Press, 1995.

ARTICLES

NATIONAL GEOGRAPHIC

Hodgson, Bryan. "Antarctica: A Land of Isolation No More." April 1990, 3–51.
Oeland, Glenn. "Emperors of the Ice." March 1996, 53–71.
Parfit, Michael. "Reclaiming a Lost Antarctic Base." March 1993, 110–126.
Scott, Sir Peter. "The Antarctic Challenge." April 1987, 538–560.
Stevens, Jane Ellen. "Exploring Antarctic Ice." May 1996, 36–53.

NEWSWEEK

Hayden, Thomas, and Sharon Begley. "Cold Comfort." August 1, 1997, 62–63.

SCIENCE NEWS

Monastersky, R. "The Antarctic Dilemma: Blowing in the Wind." February 24, 1996, 117.
———. "Antarctic Ozone Level Reaches New Low." October 16, 1993, 247.
———. "Giant Lake Hides Beneath Antarctica's Ice." June 29, 1996, 407.
———. "Ozone Hole Starts Strong, Fades Quickly." October 19, 1996, 246.
Raloff, Janet. "Giant Iceberg Breaks off Antarctica." April 29, 1995, 271.

TIME

Linden, Eugene. "Antarctica: Warning From the Ice." April 14, 1997, 55–59.

WORLD WIDE WEB

Antarctica is one of the best-covered, most interesting scientific subjects for students to study on the World Wide Web. Many sites are designed for teachers and students and allow visitors to see and hear Antarctic animals and contact Antarctic researchers. The sites are constantly changing. You can search for files with the keyword: Antarctica. Or you can begin your search at one of the following web sites:

LIVE FROM ANTARCTICA II

http://quest.arc.nasa.gov/antarctica2/

This site is a special educational program funded by the National Science Foundation. It is designed specifically for students and teachers. From January to March 1997, the site featured live video and reports from researchers in Antarctica. It continues to have teacher's guides, pictures, video clips, and dozens of links.

SIGHTS AND SOUNDS OF ANTARCTICA

http://www.webdirectory.com/antarctica/

This site, created by wildlife sound recordist and artist Doug Quin, has Quin's personal journal entries about his Antarctic visit, plus sounds and photos of glaciers, seals, penguins, and more.

NATIONAL SCIENCE FOUNDATION

http://www.nsf.gov/home/polar/

This site provides updates on what researchers are doing in Antarctica.

The Antarctica Project
P.O. Box 76920
Washington, DC 20013

Telephone: (202) 544-0236
E-mail: antarctica@igc.org
World Wide Web: www.asoc.org

This is the only nongovernmental organization in the world that works exclusively on Antarctica issues. It has fact sheets and a list of resources, including videos, posters, maps, books, and scientific papers.

INDEX

Page numbers in *boldface italics* refer to illustrations.

Adélie penguins, *30*, 57, 58
Africa, 5, *28*, 29
albatrosses, 39, 51
algae, 31, 33, 58
Amundsen, Roald, 22
Amundsen-Scott Station, 15–16
Antarctic Convergence, 19
Antarctic Peninsula, 12, 25, 57
Antarctic Treaty System, 52–54
Arctic, 10
Asia, 5, 7, 29
aurora australis, *20*, 22, 24
aurora borealis, 24
Australia, 5, 7, *28*, 29

baleen whales, 41
blue whales, 41
brine, 19

calving, 16
chlorofluorocarbons (CFCs), 25
climate, 9, 12, 19, 21, 22, 57–58
climatologists, 46
Conlan, Kathy, 49
continents, 5, *6*, 7
Convention on the Regulation of Antarctic Mineral Resource Activities, 52
Cook, Captain James, 38
crabeater seals, 39, 41, 43, 53
crèche, 39
Cretaceous period, *28*
crevasses, *16*, 17
cyclones, 26

elephant seals, 38, 39, *40–41*, 53
elevation, 12, 15
emperor penguins, *36*, 38, 39
Eurasia, *28*
Europe, 5, 7

firn, 17
fish, 9, 33, 35, 37, 51
fogbows, 24
food chain chart, *42*
fossils, 26, *27*, 29
frazil ice, 17
fulmars, 39
fur seals, 38, 39, 53

glaciers, 10, *16*, 17
global warming, 57, 58
Gondwana, 29
grease ice, 17
Greater (East) Antarctica, 12
greenhouse gases, 46
guano, 33
gulls, 39

halos, 24

ice, 9–10, 15–19, 45–46, 57–58
icebergs, 10, *14*, 16–17, 58
ice cores, 46
ice fish, 35, 37, 51
ice floes, 18
ice sheets, 17
ice shelves, 58
India, 29

katabatic wind, 25, *26*
killer whales, 41
krill, 33, *34*, 35, 41, 43, 58

Lake Vostok, 18–19
leopard seals, 39, 41, 53
Lesser (West) Antarctica, 12
lichens, 31, *32*, 33
liverworts, 33

marsupials, 29
meteorites, 46–47
midge, 33
mining, 51–52, 54
mites, 33
mosses, 33
Mt. Erebus, *8*, 9

North America, 5, 7, *28*
northern lights, 24
Notothenioids, 35, 37

overfishing, 51
ozone layer, 25

paleontologists, 26
pancake ice, 18
Pangaea, 5, 29
Panthalassa, 5
parasites, 33

Patagonian toothfish, 51
penguins, 9, *30*, 31, 33, *36*, 38–39, 49, 57, 58, *59*
petrels, 39, 51
photosynthesis, 33
phytoplankton, 25, 33, 35, 41
plants, 31, *32*, 33
Pointy Hill, *44*
pollution, 19, *48*, 49, 51–52
precipitation, 25
Protocol on Environmental Protection, 52–54

rockhopper penguins, 37
Ross seals, 39, 53

scientific research, 45–47, 49, 52–54, 58
Score, Roberta, 46
Scott, Robert, 22
seals, 9, 33, 35, 38, 39, *40–41*, 41, 53, 58
skuas, 39
South America, 5, 7, 10, *28*, 29
Southern (Antarctic) Ocean, 10, 26, 58
southern lights, 22, 24
sperm whales, 41
springtails, 33
stars, 47, 49
subantarctic, 10
sun pillars, 24

tectonic plates, 5, 6
temperature, 12, 21, 57
terns, 39
tourism, 9, 45, 49, 54
Transantarctic Mountains, 12

ultraviolet rays, 25

Vinson Massif, 12
volcanoes, 5, *8*, 9

waves, *24*, 26
Weddell seals, 39, 53
whales, 9, 33, 35, 38, 41, 43, 58
wind, 12, 24–26

zooplankton, 35